THE COMMON SENSE
Handbook

An "ordinary" Christian's perspective on handling life's twist and turns

By Dan Fleming

Foreword

Let me establish something right out of the gate. Am I perfect? Absolutely not. Do I always use common sense? Absolutely not. Have I screwed up in each of the areas presented in this book? You bet. Have these "screw ups" helped me to become wiser, more humble, and a better decision maker? Well, if not, then I don't have much common sense!

You hear it or say it from time to time. "Do you have any common sense?" "Does he or she have any common sense?" Chances are you've muttered it under your breath after dealing with someone or experiencing something that entered your path of life. Matter of fact, I've said it to my own children. "You have no common sense!"

So…..what is it? You probably know some of the more typical definitions. Off the top of my head: "using good judgment", "making good decisions", "wisdom", and on and on. Using common sense is a sign of a humble and intelligent person, it helps keep "the wrinkles" out of life, and at the very least can help keep you out of trouble!

Why then, does it seem that there are so many times that people just seem not to use it? Most of the time it's selfishness. Maybe they are in a hurry. Maybe they don't have the energy or time it takes. Or, maybe, just maybe, they have never been taught what common sense "looks like"!

Full disclosure: This book has been written by an "ordinary Joe" who has Christian beliefs and a strong faith in God. My perspective may be totally different than yours and I certainly do not expect you to agree with everything that you are about to read. And if you don't, by all means, write a book! But, when you strip away every part of your life that truly doesn't matter – fame, fortune, status, etc. – I think you will find that we are ALL extremely ordinary!

My main purpose in writing this book is to reintroduce common sense. Maybe by reading it, you will think twice before that next important decision, or reaction, or social media post, or whatever it is that requires plain old-fashioned good thinking that doesn't have only *your* best interests in mind. I also hope that reading this book causes you to nod your head (up and down) repeatedly and maybe even produces a chuckle or two! You will notice that some sections are short and to the point, while others have more details or examples – probably a result of my own life experiences.

So, without further ado, take a deep breath, turn the page, and start thinking about basic humanity!

Being a Decent Human Being

I start here because being a good person is at the heart of having common sense. Much of what you do sets the stage for your own life. Perhaps more importantly though, your actions create a ripple effect that others can ride like a gentle wave or a giant tsunami!

Treat others with respect. One of my biggest turn-offs is dealing with someone who has a big ego. The world and God have a way of humbling you when you start to feel you are more important than others. My grandfather was a good man and a successful man. He had many great qualities. He passed away many years ago. What do I remember the most out of all his qualities? He treated all people as his equal, regardless of their financial status, career, past history, etc. He understood that God created all of us and that each of us are here to serve a purpose.

Don't judge others or gossip. Have you ever been talking with a friend or group of friends and one starts being critical of someone who is not present, but is supposedly a friend as well? Or have you ever listened to your boss criticize someone behind his or her back that is supposed to be on "the same team"? It doesn't take long for you to 1) realize that person is probably talking about you when he or she has the opportunity, and 2) lose trust in that individual. Only God has the right to judge or condemn someone because He created that person and knows their circumstances. *I believe people judge or gossip because it helps them feel better about their own issues or weaknesses.*

Be kind and patient. *There exists in every interaction you have with every single person an opportunity for kindness.* Picture this: You are speeding on the interstate because, like most everyone, you have had a stressful morning full of unexpected events. A car passes you with a blinker on. Another human being has had a morning similar to yours and wants to "squeeze" in front of you because he or she is late to work. *Scenario A*: You think to yourself: "What is this jerk doing?! He is not more important than me!" You hit the gas, beep the horn, and throw a gesture up at the person so he cannot pass you and experiences your displeasure. You are now feeling more anxious and angry as a result. *Scenario B*: You think to yourself: "Wow! This person must be having a worse morning than I. Let me help him or her along." You ease off the gas, motion the person over, and give a gentle wave. You feel good about yourself because you just showed the love and patience to someone else that God shows you every day. Common sense, right? This is just one example of thousands of opportunities that will arise during your lifetime in which you can show kindness over hatred and reap the benefits of choosing to do the right thing.

Surprise! People trust and admire others who are kind, trustworthy, and non-judgmental! It's much of the basis for love and friendship! And, most likely, it will be your legacy!

Good Leadership

Are you a leader? The answer, which may surprise you, is likely YES! If you are a parent, an older sibling, a coach, a teacher, a supervisor, a committee member, or someone who has the ability to change any part of their surroundings, then you are a leader!

A leader is not simply someone with power. I've certainly had so-called "leaders" or supervisors who possessed power or the responsibility to "lead" but had absolutely no idea how to do so. You have likely had a similar experience. *A leader is someone who uses resources (human, physical, and/or capital) to positively create change that results in a desired outcome. The leader not only succeeds at a mission, but produces positive changes in others along the way.*

Here are some of the key differences between effective and ineffective leaders:

Effective Leaders	Ineffective Leaders
Lead by example	Use authority and intimidation to accomplish objectives
Motivate others to become better people and workers	Display an ego that is apparent to others
Create an atmosphere of trust and teamwork	Do not collaborate with or value the opinions of others
Emit a positive energy that is contagious to others	Are not passionate about or truly vested in the assigned mission
Experience success by achieving organizational or family goals and by being a change agent for others	Have selfish priorities not related to moving the team or mission in a positive direction

Those in leadership positions will be fondly remembered by the way they have touched or made a positive impact on others. It's as simple as that. Do not choose to lead if you only desire to achieve a certain status or salary. Choose to lead because you have a genuine passion for the assignment. God has placed specific passions in our hearts to help us determine our paths in life. *Even Jesus, the greatest leader that will ever walk this Earth, came to serve, not to be served.*

Teaching and Coaching

Teaching and coaching are arguably the two most important jobs that exist. While it pales in comparison to the role of parenting, teachers and coaches not only educate but instill foundational values and proper decision-making skills in our youth. Why then, you ask, do today's children seem to be so self-absorbed? In today's ultra-competitive world, school districts are choosing to ramp up rigor and academic standards for all students. Kids are taking classes years ahead of when my generation took them. What's the problem with developing smart children that can compete for jobs? To me it's quite simple. First, schools are no longer teaching social skills and manners because it interferes with academic time. Students do not understand how they are supposed to address, react to, or act towards different people. Throw in the fact that many districts have decided to use technology, almost exclusively, which provides students with far less opportunity to learn and develop social skills. Second, consistently high expectations are creating a new level of anxiety in our children. Mental health issues are more prevalent in children today than ever before.

What can teachers and coaches do to combat this?

1. **Look for opportunities to embed social learning in your lessons.** Give students chances to talk and debate, then provide constructive feedback.

2. **Model expected behaviors all the time.** Your actions speak louder than words. Show kindness, respect, compassion, acceptance, and understanding to your students, then acknowledge them when they do the same to you or others.

3. **<u>Expect students and athletes to mess up</u>**. Making mistakes is an important part of the learning process, whether in the classroom or on the playing field. Your reactions to their mistakes have a HUGE impact on children. Encourage them to take risks, then provide constructive feedback when they mess up! Most of us have witnessed the middle school coach berating the 12-year-old when he or she misses a shot. And as if this isn't demoralizing enough, the coach does it loudly in front of everyone! Ugh! What a terrible example and confidence killer!

4. **Be positive and energetic**. Your outlook and energy are contagious to those around you! A positive learning environment is your responsibility. Throughout my 15 years of teaching, I heard teachers say things such as "These kids are so bad!" or "These kids couldn't care less!". Then *do* something about it! You are the paid adult and it is *your* responsibility! Thank goodness so many of our teachers and coaches truly care about their students and want to make a difference in their lives! Children naturally have a positive outlook on life. Use that to your advantage by fostering their curiosity and providing opportunities for success in your lessons. Students can and will develop a love of learning because of your behaviors and the type of activities you plan. Provide fun opportunities (as appropriate) that motivate and engage students in learning. If you are having second thoughts about teaching or coaching, that likely means you do not, or no longer have, the passion necessary to be great. Here is a chance, as mentioned in the Foreword of this book, to nod your head up and down. Ready? Nod your head if you once had a teacher or coach that had no passion for his or her job and

was simply going through the motions. Yep, that's what I thought…

5. **Show them you care**. If you have ever been a classroom teacher, you already know that <u>relationships are crucial</u>. Oh, I realize that students can still learn if you do not develop a relationship with them. But if students trust you and believe you care, they will take risks and work much harder for you AND for themselves! They will open up to you and the concepts you are teaching. One of the reasons I chose to become a teacher was because of those teachers who made a big impression on me. Never underestimate the amount of influence you have on children!

One final piece of advice for teachers and coaches: Avoid politics, gossip, and negative coworkers! It will reduce your energy and enthusiasm. Focus on your students and the love for what you do!

Parenting

This chapter, if you have children, is the most important one in the book. Read it, study it, ponder it, reflect on it, and develop your own set of values and beliefs. It's the most important job in your life, will take the most energy, and will set the stage for generations to come. *This is _my_ parenting philosophy.* If you don't agree with it, develop your own. No, seriously! Get a sheet of paper and pencil out and write your own parenting philosophy! You will be a better parent as a result!

Be the person you want your kids to become. If you are affectionate, your kids will become affectionate. If you are selfish, your kids will become selfish. If you are kind and giving, your kids will become kind and giving. If you use foul language, expect the same from your kids! Make a list of the traits you most want your children to possess. If you are at a loss, start with learning about Jesus.

Spend time with your children, independently and as a family. I LOVE beach vacations! The sand, the surf, the ice cream, the summer sun – all of it! But what I love the most is the opportunity for us to be a family and to forget everything else! Make time for activities that are planned and spontaneous. My 7- year-old daughter loves to play board games. And play. And play. And play. Part of that is because she enjoys games, but more so she craves time with her family. *The bonds you form with your children while they are young will keep them close to you for the rest of their lives.*

Tell them you love them and compliment them when they deserve it. Make time each day to let your kids know how much they mean to you. Being a kid isn't as easy as it used to be, with all kinds of pressures coming from every direction. They need to feel loved and secure. Your home should provide a "safe zone" and feeling of belonging for them. Focus on what they do right, instead of what they do wrong. If you want more of a certain behavior, make a big deal of it when they exhibit that particular behavior! I'm not saying your kids shouldn't be punished or criticized for doing wrong. Just make sure you spend more time building them up than tearing them down.

Set limits on screen time. Don't use television or video games as a babysitter for your child. I repeat – *don't* use television or video games as a babysitter for your child! Set a timer if you have one. I recommend a maximum of 60 minutes per day for video games. I won't get into the reasons why video games are bad for children but encourage you to do your own research. Select television shows that have family values or an impactful message built in. We occasionally like to do "family movie night" where we sit together as a family and enjoy an uplifting movie. I'm not saying everything your child watches has to be 100% wholesome (we love superhero movies). Just be sure to pay attention to and abide by movie ratings. When kids lose their innocence, they don't get it back! If you're a Netflix fan or a cord-cutter, try Pure Flix!

Attend church consistently with your children. Children can develop a relationship with Jesus at an early age. He will place a peace inside their hearts that will shield them from the many troubled times that lay ahead. By praying and getting to know our Lord, children will develop an early understanding of the real meaning of life. If you've never been to church or if you've never taken your kids, please do. Church programs give children the opportunity to develop spiritually, make new Christian friends, allow them to serve God through community projects, teach them the importance of serving others, and much, much more.

Don't turn their lives in to a "rat race". There are lots of sports and extracurricular activities available to kids. I recommend having your children select one activity per season. If you choose to do more than that, you will notice the quality of your lives decrease. You will struggle with complicated schedules and find your family rushing to be somewhere all the time. Quality time at the dinner table will rarely occur. Kids will hurry to finish homework. Family time will take a hit. Kids will feel overwhelmed and won't have time to, well, just be kids! Plus, by focusing on less activities, they can devote more time to excelling and improving at the ones they do play!

Be a parent, not a friend. Parents discipline. Friends do not. Parents establish rules. Friends do not. *Make sure you are consistent with rules you set and the way you discipline.* Inconsistent rules and punishments send mixed messages, create uncertainty, and cause hard feelings. Kids want structure in their lives, and, in order to be effective, it needs to be predictable and firm. Younger children tend to do better with a daily routine that includes such things as the same bedtime, the same mealtime, the same time for completing homework, etc.

Admit your mistakes and apologize when you mess up. I've screwed up many times as a parent. I know for a fact I've been too hard on my kids at times, maybe didn't give them enough attention, or didn't trust them when I should have. What's the one thing I always do? Admit I made a mistake and apologize to them! Parents are human beings too. We are not perfect. And guess what? Our children know it! It establishes a double standard when *you* don't take the "high road" but expect *them* to. My son is a teenager which, of course, makes things interesting from time to time. My goal is to always maintain that special father and son bond. Part of maintaining his respect is to apologize and explain my behavior when he sees me slide off the rails! It's like pressing a "RESET" button on any issues we have with each other.

Technology

This is the section that you will most likely disagree with me. I believe that technology has a definite place in our lives, in education, and in business. I also believe that it is used for the wrong reasons as much as it is used for the right reasons.

Most of the world likes Facebook and other social media sites. I've seen quite a few people who simply can't control themselves on social media. Social media can be a wonderful tool for sharing information, staying up-to-date with friends and family, and spreading a positive message. I will never establish a personal account on a social media site. Before you call me a prude, or old, or an idiot, let me explain. Too many times I have seen people use social media to gossip, start fights, spread false information, and spy on people. But what I dislike the most is when I see people use social media to constantly post about themselves and pretend they are someone they are not. Reality check! No one needs or wants to know what you are doing every minute of the day and how wonderful you are! Stop trying to impress people and just live *your* life! Imagine the impact on our world if people used social media only for the *right* reasons!

You know it's time to get your child a cell phone when he or she may have a real need to reach *you*. Just because their friends have it does not qualify as a valid reason. Cell phones are a major distraction to children. I taught middle school for years. At first, the public-school system set a policy in which cell phones were not allowed in schools. Then not allowed to be carried but kept in lockers. Then they could be carried if turned off and were not being used during class time. Then they could be carried and turned on, as long as the phones were not being used during class unless the student was truly using it for learning purposes. (FYI - This is what I actually agree with.) Here's the catch. None of the policies were ever enforced by the school administration, which created a major battle between students, parents, and teachers. Guess who loses the battle? Yes, the teacher! As a result, many schools now have students who use their cell phones whenever they feel like it, to text, take unapproved pictures, post to social media, etc. Why? Two reasons: First, teachers are tired of fighting (and losing) this battle. Second, parents are providing cell phones to children who don't truly need a phone, *or* not establishing clear rules and protocol for using phones, *or* not punishing their children when they are inappropriately using their cell phones. I know I sound negative. Remember, I'm in favor of children having cell phones in school, when they are used appropriately and as a tool for learning.

Know what your children are doing on the computer or on their phones. It is your right and responsibility as a parent. Know your children's passwords or establish one password for the family. Ask what they are up to and what sites they are visiting. Check their history. If you think you are being nosey, well, good. You are protecting your child from many crazy things. Identity thieves, pedophiles, and pornography are just a few of the things that live on the internet!

Check to see how frequently your children's schools are using technology. Not enough and your children will not be prepared for 21st century careers. Too much and your children will not develop important social skills. Many school districts today believe they are "top notch" because they use technology all day, every day. Don't buy it. It is hurting your child's ability to converse and develop relationships with others. And, believe it or not, kids get sick of using technology *all* the time!

Set limits for *yourself.* If you love being on the internet for various reasons, set a schedule that doesn't interfere with work or your family. Don't sacrifice time with others or opportunities to better yourself as a person because you have developed an addiction to technology. <u>And it is an addiction</u>. Here are a couple examples I'm sure you can relate to. *Example 1:* An entire family is eating a meal at a restaurant. All family members are looking at their phones instead of sharing time with each other. *Example 2:* An individual is checking out at your local store and does not have the common courtesy or decency to get off the phone long enough to check out and show the cashier a little respect and kindness. Come on, people! Use some common sense! People actually find you quite disrespectful!

Driving

In honor of the movie *Groundhog Day* with Bill Murray: Don't drive angry! Had to get that out of my system…

Buckle up. Don't speed. Keep a safe distance between you and the car in front of you. Use your turn signals. Don't drink and drive. You are familiar with the standard list of safe driving laws. At least I hope you are! I am more interested in writing about driving etiquette. It should be common sense but, apparently, it's not!

When you are driving on the interstate, did you know the left lane is considered the passing lane or "fast lane"? I am amazed at how many people creep along in the passing lane with no regard for the person behind them who is trying to pass. Only drive in the left lane if you are attempting to go around someone in the right lane. If you are in the left lane and see someone in your rear-view mirror trying to get around you, please move to the right lane!

Have you ever noticed that the people who pull out in front of you tend to be the same people who are *not* in a hurry? Why would you pull out in front of someone then go below the speed limit? If you are not in a hurry, then don't pull out in front of someone! Ahhhh…feels good to let that go.

Lastly, be a patient, graceful, and forgiving driver. Show others courtesy by allowing them out of a parking lot if traffic is backed up. Try not to get mad at someone if you feel they disrespected you by cutting you off, butting in front of you, etc. Have a Christian attitude and look for ways to display it. Grace and kindness are contagious and could save your and others lives!

Friendship

There is a big difference between a "friend" and an "acquaintance". Here are several:

Acquaintance	Friend
Occasionally happen to run into	Text AND TALK TO on a regular basis
Know from a previous experience	Trust and respect
Text or contact on social media once in a while	Can be frank and honest with at the expense of hurt feelings
Seems to be a friend only when that person can benefit from knowing you	Can talk to about anything including the most private aspects of your life and sins you have committed
Comes and goes in your life	Does not judge you or gossip about you

Imagine if everyone on Facebook that sent you a "friend request" really wanted to be a *true* friend. You would have an endless support system of people that would meet all of your needs and vice versa. Sounds rather utopian doesn't it?

The truth is, REAL friends are rather hard to come by. For me, a person's character goes a long way in determining if that person is a true friend. I know that sounds judgmental but hear me out. Do you want to be someone's friend that spends a lot of time gossiping, or cheating on his or her spouse, or talks to you when it's convenient, or ignores you when other people are around? I'm in no way saying that you shouldn't be kind or "friendly" to this person. That's part of being a Christian. What I am saying is that we tend to use the word *friend* too loosely.

It seems the older I get the less I need certain types of people in my life. People that are not genuine or authentic are at the top of my list. These types of people pretend they are someone they are not, or pretend they are your friend when other people are not around. These people act totally different towards you in a social gathering.

Right now, other than my wife and most family members, I only have a few people in my life that I believe do not judge me, do not gossip about me, are there for me anytime I need them, and are very authentic. Now being very honest with yourself, how many do you have? If it's more than just a few, that's awesome. Reach out to those people and let them know they are true friends. They are priceless in your life!

This leads me to another aspect of friendship. If you make a list of qualities you expect a true friend to have, well, this "person" would have to be pretty darn perfect. Right? You would hold this person to a very high standard. *This person would always love you, always forgive you, always listen to you, always want the best for you, and never forsake you.* If you have not already done so, let me suggest that you make Jesus your best friend. When others are not there for you, He always is. Anytime you need Him. And while you may not always understand or agree with His answers or decisions, He will always do what is best for you. In order for this to happen, you have to open your heart and allow Him to enter. Just like a regular friendship, you must develop and nurture a relationship with Him. It is exponentially and eternally worth the efforts!

Lastly, if you are a true friend, you will confront someone when you see him or her going down the wrong path. A true friend will "call people out" when they are doing wrong! I know it takes a lot of nerve! But it would (and should) take even more nerve to allow your friend to do something that will hurt him/herself or someone else. So, be careful how you say it, BUT SAY IT!

Family

A family is the most important support structure for all of us. I am not merely talking about your immediate family, but your entire family. Cousins, grandparents, aunts, uncles, in-laws – everyone. A properly functioning family loves one another (and shows it), supports one another, trusts one another, defends one another, makes sacrifices for one another, and finds ways to spend time together. While Jesus should be our spiritual rock, our family should be our earthly rock. Being in the midst of family should be our safe place where we are accepted despite our faults (within reason).

All families have their share of ups and downs. Enjoy the ups and tread lightly on the downs. I can "get real" very quickly with people that are being disrespectful or immoral. I will not go to this level with my family. Why? Simple. They are my family. They deserve my best in both easy and difficult situations. Overreacting causes hard feelings and leads to emotional scars. If you have a "falling out" with one family member, you will feel the ripple effects across the entire family. When the scars begin to add up, here come the problems! Families start communicating less, start drifting apart, and stop feeling safe with each other. As time goes on, an awkwardness develops over unresolved issues. The next thing you know, you have one heck of a mess! I once worked with an individual who seemed like she was constantly "writing off" her family members. First, it was her siblings. Then her husband. Then her second husband. One bad argument and she was done! No wonder she seemed to be an emotional mess most of the time!

Always be supportive, genuine, and sincere with your family. Be honest with each other. Don't let family members go down the wrong path. Sometimes the truth will hurt, but it needs to be heard. Give advice and constructive criticism with gentle words that come from your heart and are spoken out of love.

Look for ways to nourish your relationships and strengthen the bonds you have with each other. What happened to family reunions? You know, the ones where you would inevitably have your cheeks pinched as a child? Even though I only saw some of those family members once a year, I loved going to those zany family reunions. It gave me what many people do not have, an identity and a sense of belonging.

I believe that many of the emotional problems that people are experiencing today are the result of not having a close family, or having a broken family resulting from a divorce or a falling out. I also believe that, in general, people focus on family less than ever. <u>It is hard to build a strong life on a weak foundation</u>. And those ingredients for a strong foundation are faith, family, and friends.

Public Education

There are five areas I am focusing on within public education: student character, technology, "dead weight", class sizes, and safety. I chose these topics because I think they are not specific to just a few schools but are an issue to the vast majority of public schools.

Our focus on academics, a fast-paced curriculum, and high stakes testing has left little time to teach children manners and character traits such as respect, generosity, responsibility, and etiquette. We are turning students into "learning machines" with minimal social skills and values. This is a real shame. To put it bluntly, Jesus prefers that His followers possess Christian values and good character traits over mastering a curriculum. I understand that students need the skills and knowledge to compete in a ferociously competitive job market. We are starting to see a definite fracture in our social structure. You can be very intelligent and prepared to enter a certain career, but if you are lacking the right character traits, social skills, and an engaging personality, you are likely not going to get the job you want or be successful at it. One of the hallmarks of a declining civilization is when there is more of a focus on personal power and success and less on family and personal virtues. If you want to see evidence of a decrease in character expectations, take a look at how students are permitted to act in school hallways during a class change, or in the cafeteria. A fair share of students is not displaying character or monitoring their own behaviors. I don't mean to stereotype all public schools with this, but I do believe it is more the norm than the exception.

I'm all for schools to use technology at opportune times during the school day. Students can create and share work with teachers and other students, even across the state or nation. Students can use their imagination and creativity to develop projects and other assignments that would not be possible without technology. Students can learn from each other and acquire information at lightning speed. I would caution educators to 1) not overuse technology, 2) always be aware of what students are doing when using technology, and 3) make sure appropriate filters are on all devices. I worked in a school where technology was used so much that students got sick of it! They were begging for pencil and paper assignments, and activities that allowed them to have discussions with each other. Students want and need to talk to each other to develop social skills. Teachers should circulate through the classroom to make sure students are not visiting inappropriate websites or use some type of data monitoring system so they know what students are up to. I have seen fights in school resulting from social media posts that occurred during class time. Filters should be in place that block students from visiting sites that are inappropriate or not pertinent to the lesson. You cannot expect all children to be mature and responsible enough not be lured by all the temptations of the internet. They are children! <u>Schools should set strict appropriate-use policies for technology and make students abide by them.</u>

I think we can all agree that each school district has its share of "dead weight", or teachers that are burnt out or not passionate about working with children. They give minimum effort, lay low, give assignments that do not require much effort in regard to planning and grading, and are looking to collect a paycheck and wait on retirement. Why are these teachers in our schools? Don't administrators notice their lack of effort and dedication? Well, most of these teachers are in our schools thanks to unions. While I'm not totally opposed to unions, I do believe they wrongly protect weak teachers. And, yes, administrators do know who their weak teachers are. The majority of administrators are not willing to engage in the battle involving placing a teacher on an improvement plan or moving a teacher out of the classroom. Kudos to the administrators who are willing to do the right thing and demand our teachers give their best to our children.

I'll never forget my third year of teaching. I had thirty-seven 8th grade students of all abilities and personalities jammed into my classroom. I even had one sitting at my desk so I could fit everyone in the room! Now don't get me wrong. I loved this class. They always kept me guessing and all those personalities meant there was never a dull moment. None of these students were considered "advanced" learners. That left me with the responsibility of trying to meet the needs and different learning styles (and manage the behaviors) of 37 students, by myself. This should not have happened and should not still be happening to teachers today. Teachers cannot ensure that all students in very large classes are learning all skills being taught. Common sense, right? Apparently not. In situations like this, teachers and students are being setup for failure. Even by grouping students according to skill deficiencies and learning styles, it is very hard to create a successful learning environment when class sizes get above 25, and that's based on the assumption that there are no behavior issues! I encourage you to check on the size of your child's classes and what support staff are placed in his or her classes.

I believe safety is going to be the biggest issue in our public schools moving forward. Even more important than test data! If schools and governments want our students to perform during academic testing, our students need to feel and be safe. A consensus needs to be reached on how this is going to happen and it needs to be included in school district or federal budgets every year moving forward. The biggest weapon against violence is free. It's called diligence. Teachers, students, resource officers, and other stakeholders must be diligent about noticing and reporting possible threats. <u>If you see something unusual, report it</u>. This could be something subtle such as a change in behavior or a social media post that seems out of line. I am not in favor of arming teachers. I cannot imagine many of my former colleagues carrying a weapon! Don't get me wrong. They were wonderful teachers but did not possess the mental capability to point a gun and pull the trigger! Teachers are compassionate, caring, and loving people who likely prefer not to carry a gun. I am in favor of each school having a resource officer assigned to a certain part of the building or number of students. This officer should have a very defined role in the building that includes regularly monitoring various areas, getting to know students, talking with school counselors about concerns, and even leading mentoring sessions with students. I also believe each school should have one location where people enter and exit during the school day. That location should have metal detectors and be manned by at least one very diligent administrator or officer. You cannot place a price on the safety of our children. Don't accept that excuse from your Board of Education. If funds are "not available" they should be rerouting them from other projects or initiatives of less importance. And they should be doing it without delay.

Finding Your Passions

Life seems to have a much greater purpose and be far easier and more fulfilling when you realize your passions and engage in them. As I stated earlier, I believe God has placed unique passions in our heart. Those passions help us to complete the missions that God has secretly assigned us in our lives. Without identifying or engaging in your passions, your life will likely feel dull and meaningless.

Some of my passions include teaching, traveling and vacationing with my family, construction, animals, and football. When I spend time at these activities it seems like all is right with the world. I am happier, have more energy, and am "in the zone"!

I encourage you to choose one of your passions when deciding on a career or a career change. There are not many things worse than spending years at a job that you are not happy with or passionate about. It zaps your energy and enthusiasm each day, even though you likely haven't given "your all" in being successful at it! Again, I think this is God's way of showing you that He had bigger plans for you than a job that you did not want or like. When you have a job you love, you will notice 1) days go fast, 2) you are motivated to get to work and work hard, 3) you are making a big difference in the mission of the organization, and 4) you are being promoted.

One word of caution about your passions. Do not place them above God. I remember my pastor saying "Whatever you devote the most time doing is your god." Time for a confession. At one time, I was totally out of control with fantasy football. I would study and read as much as I could, preparing for draft day. I would spend hours, day after day, month after month, studying player stats to make sure I had the best team possible. Out. Of. Control. Nowadays, I still love playing fantasy football. But it is a hobby instead of a religion. So, please, learn to manage your passions. They can steal large portions of your life and develop into sicknesses if you do not learn to control them!

Take some time to make a list of the things you are passionate about then be honest with yourself. Are you spending too much time or not enough time on them? If you really don't have any passions, ask God to help you identify your passions and present a path or opportunity that allows you to engage in them in a way that brings Glory to Him.

Fear

Fear is the root of hatred and division. It is based on an uncertainty of an outcome or set of outcomes. How many things were you afraid of earlier in your life only to realize that your fear was unwarranted after you learned more about the thing you were afraid of?

In my opinion, it's much of the reason racism exists. People are afraid of those people, places, events, and possibilities that they have no knowledge of. Their ignorance translates to fear which then translates to hatred.

Our fears put limits on our abilities to grow as people. We prefer to live in our "comfort zones" where we are not forced to take any risks or encounter any uncertainty. We want to feel like we are always in control of our lives and fear takes away the control we perceive we have.

Were you ever forced to face one of your fears, only to find there was nothing to be afraid of after all? Matter of fact, maybe you were presently surprised by how much you enjoyed the person, place, or thing that you were scared of.

Fear and anxiety can steal your energy and prevent you from fulfilling your potential and purpose in life. <u>The easiest way to not worry or be afraid is to have faith and trust in God</u>. Having faith in God allows you to let go of your fears and anxiety. Ask Him to take away your fears and anxiety. This took me a long time to realize and accept. My life became a lot easier when I handed control, the control I never truly had in the first place, over to God.

I would encourage you to do two things regarding your fears. First, make a list of them and identify why you are afraid or worried about each of them. If you cannot identify a reason for your fear, perhaps you should not be afraid! Sometimes we "inherit" fears from our family simply based on their perspective or experiences. Examine your fears closely to see which are warranted. I think you may be surprised!

Second, stop worrying. No seriously, you are wasting your time and energy! Instead of worrying, resolve it! Maybe it's an awkward situation at work, a suspected health issue, a loss of employment, or an impending home foreclosure. Instead of sitting around worrying, take action and do your best to fix things! After this, give it to God and pray that He will handle it for you. He may not give you the solution you wanted but you must learn to accept His will.

Money

We all need a certain amount of money in order to survive. It seems like there are always bills to pay, and unexpected expenses. We do well when we establish budgets, live within our means, and learn to control our spending.

We get in trouble when we follow society's example of instant gratification. Instead of being patient and saving for what we want, we borrow money or use credit. Or we buy something, such as a house or car, that is not in line with the salary we are earning. That purchase then becomes a burden to us and hinders our ability to use the money for better purposes such as donating to charity, church offerings, or family activities.

I am a firm believer that money cannot buy happiness. Look at how many professional athletes and other celebrities have turmoil in their lives. Having lots of money does not make them immune to life's problems.

Money, power, and greed are the root of all evil. It is why corruption exists within government and society. It is why people focus more on themselves instead of serving others. It is why people are more concerned with the performance of their 401K accounts than they are with moral decency and the future of humanity. It is why people sacrifice priceless family time by spending too much time in a job they believe gives them power and prestige. And on and on.

Your top priorities with your money should be establishing a budget and focusing on eliminating your debt. Interest on mortgages and credit cards will eat your money and rob your financial independence. Two other top priorities should be giving regularly to your church or charity and contributing to your retirement account. In order to do this, you will need the discipline to give up some of the non-essential items in your life. This could include a weekly shopping trip, eating out too often, or selling that Harley Davidson or ATV sitting in your garage that requires a monthly payment.

If you have children, you should be investing in their upcoming college or trade school education. There are many options available that allow you to make automatic contributions each month. Set up the account while they are young and you will be amazed how much money has accumulated when they need it.

My point here is to spend your money wisely and for the right reasons. Do not be selfish with your money. Do not buy fancy homes or automobiles as status symbols or to impress others. Imagine how different our world would be if all people donated generously to churches, charities, and research. Imagine too if all of us put the needs of others first when determining how to spend our money. People I know that give their money generously and live modest lives seem to possess a genuine happiness that is not based on what they own, but what they give.

Be Yourself

As I wrap up this handbook, I truly hope you have found my perspective on many of these topics useful. At a minimum, I hope it has made you examine your life and your priorities and make any necessary changes that can improve your life, your relationships with family and friends, and your relationship with God.

Be true to yourself and who you really are. If you have to pretend you are someone you are not in order to impress people, then you are hanging out with the wrong people. We begin teaching children at an early age to be genuine and real. I think adults need a reminder as well. God did not design you with a distinct personality, specific interests, and certain abilities for you to hide them while you lead a fake life. Don't let others "steal" your life with the expectations they have for you. Stay on the path that allows you to fulfill *your* dreams and passions.

You are going to make mistakes in life. Lots of them. Some minor. Some major. Don't let your mistakes define you as a person. Learn from them, pray for forgiveness, and move on with your life. I believe that God allows us to mess up because it "refines" us, keeps us humble, and makes us better Christians if we learn from our mistakes.

Be a positive role model to as many as you can, as often as you can. Allow others to see your heart through the love, kindness, patience, and mercy you exhibit. Shine your light and be a difference maker in this world.

Spend your time with positive and moral people who accept you for who you are. Hold onto your Christian values and beliefs. Life is short! Grab it by the

horns and make it a better place than you found it! It's just
COMMON SENSE!